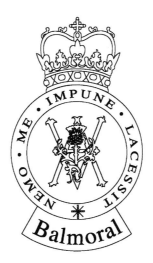

BALMORAL

Highland retreat of The Royal Family since 1852

Balmoral Castle from the North West across the River Dee - 1898
by John Campbell Mitchell (1837-1926)

Front cover: Balmoral Castle from the North side
of the River Dee by F. Colebrook Stockdale

The Queen's Piper
wearing Balmoral Tartan

Every year I seem to become fonder of this dear place, still more so, now that great and excellent taste has been stamped everywhere.

Queen Victoria

The Chamois statue
and fountain in the
rose garden

The South Facade

Lóch Muick

The Jubilee
Conservatory

*HM The Queen and
HRH The Duke of Edinburgh
attending the Braemar
Gathering, 2003, this event
has been organised by
The Braemar Royal Highland
Society for over 187 years*

*The Jubilee
Conservatory was
rebuilt to celebrate
Her Majesty
The Queen's
Golden Jubilee
in 2002*

'It was so calm and so solitary, it did one good as one gazed around; and the pure mountain air was most refreshing. All seemed to breathe freedom and peace, and to make one forget the world and its sad turmoils... the scenery all around is the finest almost I have seen anywhere.. we are certainly in the finest part of the Highlands and quite in the heart of them and the soil and climate are the driest I almost saw anywhere. You can walk for ever... and then the wildness, the solitariness of everything is so delightful, so refreshing, the people are so good and so simple...'

The Story of Balmoral

I n the autumn of 1842, two and a half years after her marriage to Prince Albert and five years after her accession to the throne, Queen Victoria paid her first visit to Scotland. The visit centred around Edinburgh; but the Queen and Prince also made a brief excursion into Perthshire, where they stayed with the Marquis of Breadalbane at Taymouth Castle. They were so struck with the Highlands that they resolved to return. Two years later they were back in Perthshire, this time as the guests of Lord and Lady Glenlyon at Blair Atholl, where they stayed for nearly three weeks. Although even more enthusiastic after this visit, they were not to see the Highlands for another three years. Then, to make a change, they went further to the west. They found the western lochs and isles, among which they sailed in the Royal Yacht for the first three days, enchanting. But after that the rain came. 'There is little to say of our stay at Ardverikie' the Queen wrote in her journal, 'the country is very fine, but the weather was most dreadful.'

Meanwhile, to the east of the Grampian Mountains, the son of Sir James Clark, her physician, had been the guest of Sir Robert Gordon in his small Deeside castle at Balmoral. Sir James received glowing accounts, not only of the scenery, but also of the climate. The air, his son reported, was of unusual dryness and purity. The Queen and the Prince must have heard these reports with mixed feelings.

Details of two portraits of Queen Victoria and Prince Albert by Winterhalter, pictured respectively in 1845 and 1850, around the time of their first visits to Scotland. The young Queen was 26 and her husband, 31.

Later the same year Sir Robert died, and, encouraged by Sir James, they seized the opportunity to negotiate for the property with his brother, the Earl of Aberdeen (until recently Foreign Secretary and later to become Prime Minister). It was held on a lease from the Earl of Fife, which had twenty-seven years to run. After searching enquiries they bought this lease on 17th February 1848 and thus, in the autumn of the same year, on Friday 8th September, they arrived to take possession of a property which they had never seen, but to which they had committed themselves for many years to come.
They were not disappointed.

Opposite:
The landscape
surounding Balmoral
is characterised by the
clear fast-flowing River
Dee and ancient
Caledonian pine forests

In her diary that evening the Queen described the 'pretty little castle in the old Scottish style' surrounded by beautiful wooded hills. It all reminded them of the landscapes in Thuringia, Germany, Prince Albert's homeland.

The old Castle, Balmoral, September 1854. A year later, the Royal Family were able to move in to their new castle 100 yards away

The core of the 'pretty little castle' was at least two centuries old, but its outward appearance was entirely due to a reconstruction carried out only 18 years earlier by Sir Robert Gordon himself. Though he did not own the land, Gordons had lived there before. The first recorded appearance of the name at Balmoral occurs in the late fifteenth century, at the same time as another branch of the family acquired neighbouring Abergeldie. The Abergeldie Gordons have remained in possession (leasing parts of their property to the Royal Family from 1850 onwards), but Balmoral passed to the Farquharson family in the seventeenth century, and from them to the Earls of Fife at the end of the eighteenth century. Both families were neighbours, the Farquharsons owning, as they still do, much of the land north of the river, and the Earls of Fife owning the estates of Mar, further up the valley. Nearly two hundred years had thus passed since a Gordon had lived at Balmoral, when Sir Robert took the lease of the property.

As the days went by, the Queen and Prince became ever more certain that they had found the ideal holiday home. 'I seldom walk less than four hours a day' wrote the Queen 'and when I come in I feel as if I want to go out again'. For the Prince, the shooting was the chief attraction and the Queen often accompanied him. For this they did not need to go far afield, as the forest was close, but sometimes they made long expeditions into the mountains. Their stay lasted three weeks. On their last day the Queen wrote 'it always gives me a pang to leave the Highlands, and this year we have been so especially happy there!!' The inhabitants of Deeside echoed their sentiments, festooning their road to the coast with banners bearing valedictory inscriptions. One urged the royal couple 'more beloved than ever, haste ye back to our home of heather'.

They resolved to do more than haste back. Soon after their return they opened negotiations for the purchase of the land on which Balmoral stood, and also for the lease and purchase of respectively the neighbouring estates of Abergeldie and Birkhall.

In November they were delighted to hear that the owners of all three properties were willing to treat. Not long afterwards Birkhall was bought in the name of The Prince of Wales, then aged seven, and Prince Albert took a long lease of Abergeldie. The negotiations with the trustees of the Earl of Fife were more protracted, and three and a half years were to pass before a price was agreed. On 22nd June 1852, the fee simple of Balmoral was purchased by Prince Albert. Meanwhile the Royal Family were able to spend six weeks at Balmoral each autumn.

The walks, the shooting and the expeditions continued, there was boating and fishing on Loch Muick (which, wrote Queen Victoria, 'means pigs, not a pretty name'), they built themselves a shiel, or mountain hut, near the loch where they could spend the night, and they attended highland gatherings. 'The place is very pretty, the house very small' Charles Greville wrote about life in the Castle in 1849, 'They live there without any state whatever . . . not merely like private gentlefolks, but like very small gentlefolks, small house, small rooms, small establishment ... They live with the greatest simplicity and ease. He shoots every morning, returns to luncheon, and then they walk and drive. She is running in and out of the house all day long, and often goes about alone, walks into the cottages, sits down and chats with the old women.'

Queen Victoria in her carriage on the shores of
Loch Muick; the loch-side house Glass-Alt-Shiel
in the background. Watercolour by William Simpson

Every time Queen Victoria and Prince Albert returned, the improvements planned the previous year awaited their inspection. In 1849 they founded a new kitchen, staff quarters and offices, and new paths beside Craig Gowan and behind the house. In 1850 there were more new paths, a venison larder and kennels, and several cottages had been built or repaired. This year also saw the first of the great series of plantations with which the Prince transformed the appearance of the valley. In 1851 there were more cottages, a pony stable, a carpenter's workshop and an ingenious prefabricated iron structure from Edward T. Bellhouse's Manchester factory to serve as a ballroom, as well as a second plantation on Craig Gowan.

During their stay in 1852 a cairn was erected on Craig Gowan to commemorate the purchase. Queen Victoria, Prince Albert and the Royal children laid stones followed by the Household and all others present. The pipes were played, whisky given to all, and reels danced during the building, which took an hour. The Prince climbed the cairn to place the last stone and three cheers were given. 'It was a gay, pretty, and touching sight' the Queen wrote, 'and I felt almost inclined to cry. The view was so beautiful ... the day so fine ... May God bless this place, and allow us yet to see and enjoy it many a long year.'

Her prayer was not to be granted. Prince Albert, then 33 was spared for only nine more years. Meantime much was accomplished.

During their four previous visits to Balmoral the Queen and Prince realised that Sir Robert Gordon's 'very small house' was no longer adequate for their needs. They had a growing family; room must be found for members of the Household in attendance; and the demands of hospitality were increasing, not only towards personal friends but also towards guests, such as Cabinet Ministers, whose presence the Queen required for reasons of State. Now that the land was theirs, they decided to rebuild.

A contemporary print showing Queen Victoria, Prince Albert and family boarding the Royal Train in London for Scotland

Queen Victoria's bedroom in the old castle

Portrait of Prince Albert painted shortly before his death in 1861. He is wearing Royal Stewart plaid and a traditional highland brooch

*A view from Craig Gowan,
looking down the valley
towards Abergeldie and Ballater,
September 1854*

The architect selected was William Smith, City Architect of Aberdeen, whose father John had reconstructed the existing building for Sir Robert Gordon. Soon after the Royal Family arrived at the Castle, Mr Smith was summoned from Aberdeen and on 8th September 1852, as the Queen noted in her diary, the Prince was occupied with him all morning.

They chose a new site 100 yards to the North West for the building, so that they could continue to occupy the old house while the new Castle was under construction. For stone, the neighbouring quarries of Glen Gelder offered a near white granite, a pleasant contrast to the sombre tones of most stone of that kind. Work progressed so well that parts of the house had risen to the second storey when the Royal Family returned in September 1853.

The new Balmoral Castle in the course of construction, Spring 1854. And below, the completed wing and tower 150 years later

Right: The new Balmoral Castle in the course of construction, Spring 1854

Compare this with the completed South Facade as it appears today

On the 28th of the month the Queen laid the foundation stone. Before it was placed in position she signed a parchment recording the date; and this, together with an example of each of the current coins of the realm, was placed in a bottle, which was inserted in a cavity below the site prepared for the stone. After the ceremony there were games, dinner and dancing for the workmen.

The Royal Family spent two seasons in the old house while the new Castle was being built, and it was ready for them when they returned to Balmoral in 1855. 'The new house looks beautiful' the Queen recorded in her diary on 7th September 1855. 'The Tower is, however, but half finished, as well as the rooms which are in the connecting wing, and the offices are still unbuilt. The Gentlemen (excepting the Minister) have to live in the old house, and so do most of the servants ... An old shoe was thrown after us, into the house, when we entered the hall . . .'. Not only was the house attractive and comfortable, but, as she wrote to her uncle Leopold, 'it has a beautiful view, which the old one had not'. In her diary she is more specific 'The view from the drawing room, and our rooms just above, of the valley looking up to the Dee with the mountains, which one could never get from the old house, is quite beautiful'.

Balmoral Castle from the opposite side of the River Dee, September 1857

By a happy coincidence, news of the fall of Sebastopol arrived three days after their entry into the new house. 'In a few minutes' wrote the Queen, 'Albert and all the Gentlemen, in every species of attire, sallied forth, followed by all the servants, and gradually the whole population of the village ... to the top of Craig Gowan, where the cairn stands. We watched, and saw the bonfire (prepared the previous year after a false report of the fall of the town) lit, accompanied by cheers. It blazed forth brilliantly, and one could see the many figures surrounding it, some dancing, all shouting, and Ross playing the pipes, Grant and McDonald continually firing off guns. Albert ... said the scene had been wild and exciting beyond everything. Healths had been drunk amidst great enthusiasm . . .'

The Crimean War on the edges of the Black Sea, involving Britain, France, Turkey and Russia, saw many acts of bravery in battles such as The Alma and Sebastopol in 1855. Prince Albert was much involved in the initiation of the Victoria Cross, Britain's highest military honour, and it was Queen Victoria who chose the inscription 'For Valour'

One of the first medals to be awarded was given to Lieutenant William Hope (right), of 7th Regiment Royal Fusiliers for his courage at Sebastopol, receiving his medal personally from Queen Victoria in Hyde Park in 1857, the year of the photograph of the Castle, above. All Victoria Crosses are made from melted down bronze guns captured at the fall of Sebastopol. The remaining ingot of metal is believed to be sufficient for a further 80 Crosses

A few days later came another happy event. Prince Frederick William of Prussia (later the Emperor Frederick III of Germany), who was staying at the house, asked for the hand of the Princess Royal, eldest child of the Queen and Prince Albert. The parents gave their consent, and the Princess accepted his proposal though as she was not yet fifteen the wedding could not take place for several years. They were married in January 1858, and a cairn was raised on Craig Canup to commemorate the occasion. Their first child was the future Kaiser Wilhelm II of Germany.

Queen Victoria's sitting room. Photograph of a watercolour by James Roberts, 1857

In the following year the new Castle was completed, and the old demolished 'The whole house has a very fine effect' the Queen noted '. . . and the little flower garden on the West side ... looks so pretty. On the wall on that side are sculptured arms of the different shields, which have very strong effect, and under my window a bas-relief representing St Hubert, with St George and St Andrew on either side all executed by Mr Thomas'. John Thomas, R.A., a sculptor much admired by Prince Albert, was subsequently engaged by him to design the interior of his model dairy in the Home Park at Windsor and the interior of the Print Room of the Royal Library at Windsor Castle.

Balmoral Castle's current cipher is taken from a decorative carving on the building produced at the inauguration of the new Castle. The Scottish thistle is intertwined with the letters 'V' and 'A'; Victoria and Albert

The Prince was no less delighted;

'The way in which the building and grounds come out gives me much pleasure and surpasses my fondest expectations. The big tower looks very imposing and the difficult excavation in front of the house looks quite natural ~ if the ground had grown in that way.'

The Main Hall with the foot of the staircase. Photograph by George Washington Wilson and Co., c.1875

The 'Big Tower'
looking equally
imposing today.
The Royal
Standard is
always flown when
HM The Queen is
in residence

He now turned his mind to dealing with the aftermath of the 'difficult excavation'. 'Albert is very busy' noted the Queen 'superintending the plantations and laying out the grounds, which no one understands as well as he does'. Later he was 'out very early, full of arrangements, orders, etc. and directions about the new stables which are being built'. When the time approached for them to leave for the South, the Queen confided to her diary 'Every year I seem to become fonder of this dear place, still more so, now that great and excellent taste has been stamped everywhere'.

On their return to Balmoral in 1857 they found the new stables completed, and a new bridge across the Dee between the Castle and Crathie designed by Brunel. This is the bridge by which visitors now approach the entrance to the Castle grounds. The Royal party drove to the Kirk over it for the first time on 13th September. It had been built to make possible the closing of that part of the South Deeside road which ran through the Balmoral Estate to the old Bridge of Dee at Invercauld, in order to give the estate greater privacy. Travellers along the Eastern part of this road were now linked by the bridge to the North Deeside road, which they could use for the stretch between Balmoral, Invercauld and Braemar. The extensive improvements to the grounds planned by Prince Albert (on whom the Queen had now conferred the title of Prince Consort) were in full progress, in accordance with a model, which he had constructed in sand. They were completed two years later, in 1859. Meanwhile the Prince turned his attention to the farms, superintending the design of new buildings at Invergelder, the main farm on the estate. They were completed in 1861.

When the Royal Family left for the South towards the end of October that year, plans had been drawn up for a new model dairy, to be built on the most up-to-date and sanitary principles like the one recently erected at Windsor. The Prince was never to see this completed. At Windsor Castle a month later he fell sick of typhoid, and three weeks afterwards he died.

Opposite: Queen Victoria erected this huge bronze by William Theed of her much beloved late husband, Prince Albert in 1867. Very much a highland impression of him, he carries a gun and is accompanied by his retriever. He wears Highland dress and the Order of the Garter

After the death of her
husband The Prince
Consort, The Queen
increasingly came to
rely on Balmoral's
strong and down-to-
earth Ghillie, John
Brown. He was to
become a very important
part of the Queen's life.

This painting by Charles
Burton Barber shows
John Brown attending a
mournful and reflective
Monarch on horseback
in her characteristic
black attire, with
Balmoral Castle in the
background.

John Brown in 1860

Queen Victoria riding 'Gordon', attended by John Brown

The Queen, though heartbroken at her loss, resolved that everything should continue as the Prince had wished. Work on the dairy went forward and as early as the following May, a season in which she had never visited Balmoral, she arrived with her second daughter, Princess Alice, to see building in progress, and to inspect a new path on Craig Gowan which the Prince had planned. She also drove to the site for the obelisk which, as her diary relates, 'the good people here have subscribed £100 at their own expense, as a memorial to their dear Master. It is very touching'.

In the 39 years that passed before the end of the Queen's long reign, little more was done, or needed to be done, to the property. The dairy was finished in the following year, and extensions made to it two years later, when a new water supply was brought to the Castle from the Gelder burn. A new mountain path was constructed where an existing one was found to be dangerous. As staff increased, new cottages were occasionally erected. One of these, called Baile na Coille, was built for the Queen's highland servant, John Brown and is now the home of the Resident Factor. Another, known as Karim Cottage, which stands by the road leading from the entrance gates to the stables, was built for the Queen's Indian secretary, the Munshi Abdul Karim, during the last years of her reign.

The Munshi Abdul Karim, and Queen Victoria, in the Garden Cottage, Balmoral, October 1894

The most noticeable additions to the landscape in the years after 1861 were the monuments. Some recorded a happy event like the cairn raised on Craig Gowan in honour of Princess Alice's marriage to the Grand-Duke Louis of Hesse-Darmstadt in July 1862. A few weeks later a second and more imposing cairn was raised on Creag Lurachain in memory of the Prince Consort. The Queen herself, with six of her children, placed stones on the foundation bearing their initials, and the structure was then raised to a height of thirty-five feet, with the outer stones (unlike those of the other cairns), smoothed and cemented. On it was inscribed:

The inscription on Prince Albert's cairn. It is interesting to note that the stone plaque is designed and angled in such a way as to make the inscription legible for the reader down below at the foot of the pyramid

To the beloved memory of Albert, the Great and Good Prince Consort, erected by his broken-hearted widow Victoria R 21st August 1862

'He being made perfect in a short time fulfilled a long time: for his soul pleased the Lord: therefore hasted He to take him away from among the wicked'

Wisdom of Solomon Chapter IV Verse 13-14.

Opposite: Prince Albert's cairn

Besides these two cairns, and that of the Princess Royal, there are four others each raised to commemorate the marriages of Queen Victoria's children - Princess Helena, Princess Beatrice, Prince Arthur and Prince Leopold.

In addition to the cairns, other monuments were erected closer to the Castle. Near the obelisk in memory of the Prince Consort, the Queen erected a huge bronze statue of the Prince described and illustrated on pages 16 and 17.

Cairn to celebrate the marriage of HRH Princess Beatrice to HRH Prince Henry Maurice of Battenburg 23rd July 1885

In due course a statue of the Queen, commemorating the golden jubilee of her reign in 1887, was to be erected opposite the statue of The Prince Consort. Behind it is an obelisk raised by the tenants and staff of the estate in memory of the Queen after her death in 1901. Not far from these monuments are two others, one a cross raised in memory of the Queen's second son, Alfred, Duke of Edinburgh and Coburg, who died in 1900, and the other a statue of John Brown, the Queen's Highland servant, who died in 1883, by Sir Edgar Boehm.

As the years went by the Queen spent longer at Balmoral. It was full of her happiest memories, and also provided the solitude, which she wanted so much. She usually went north for a month in May, and often returned for as many as three in the autumn. Her Ministers were far from pleased that she spent a third of the year at a distance of five hundred miles from the capital. Those invited to stay there were often less than comfortable, as she liked the minimum of heating, and the airs of Deeside are keener than those of the Thames Valley. They were glad to return to warmer latitudes, but for the Queen, leaving Balmoral at the end of the autumn visit was distressing.

In 1869 she wrote to Sir Theodore Martin, biographer of the Prince Consort:

'The departure from Scotland, that loved and blessed land - "The birthplace of valour, The country of worth" - was very painful and the sehnsucht [longing] for it, and proportionate disgust on returning to this gloomiest saddest of places [Windsor where the Prince Consort had died]- very great. It is not all the pure air, the quiet and the beautiful scenery, which renders it so delightful - it is the atmosphere of loving affection and hearty attachment of the people around Balmoral which warms the heart and does one good.'

When the Queen died in 1901 the property passed under the terms of her will to King Edward VII, and from him to each of his successors. The new King had more sociable inclinations, and never spent longer than a month at Balmoral, usually less. King George V had a greater affection for it, and used to go there for about eight weeks in the autumn. So did King George VI, who received a warm welcome on his first visit as king. 'The Aberdeenshire people' he wrote to his mother Queen Mary in 1937 'turned out well for our drive from Aberdeen, and we saw many friends at their own gates. When we got to the gate here, about 100 of the employees here pulled the Balmoral Victoria with us four in it and Ross on the box all the way to the Castle, except for pipers, who marched ahead playing . . . It was their own idea'. Her Majesty The Queen and her family are no less attached to Balmoral, and are in residence from early August to mid-October, and stay for occasional weekends when their duties permit.

Although Balmoral remains largely the same as it was a century ago, successive Royal owners have followed the initiative of the Prince Consort in increasing the amenities of the estate and productivity of its farms and forests. Several of the plantations devised by the Prince Consort have been felled on reaching maturity and replaced by new. Since the gale of 1953, which caused widespread damage, many hundreds of acres have been replanted.

HM The Queen and HRH The Duke of Edinburgh at Balmoral

HM The Queen and HRH The Duke of Edinburgh
attending the Estate Staff Ball in Balmoral's Ballroom

Guide to the Castle and Policies

Having passed through the main gates the visitor is confronted by a very fine and rare specimen of a Golden Nootka Cypress. The drive is flanked by evergreen conifers. The silvery boles and varied blue-grey foliage of the Noble Firs and the soft, fresh green of the young Western Hemlocks are set against the dark green of the Douglas Firs. In autumn the colour of the few beeches and birches shine out among the dark greens. The four main species in the policies (Douglas Fir, Western Hemlock, Grand Fir and Noble Fir) flower and fruit often and produce a prolific amount of natural regeneration which is managed to provide the next generation of trees. Many of the larger trees were planted in the time of Prince Albert, who laid out the drive.

The main wrought iron entrance gates were commissioned by King George V, and made by the local blacksmith, George Gillespie, who was paid £50 for his six months work. They were erected in 1925

Some of the large conifers on the main drive and in the vicinity of the cafeteria have been numbered and can be identified from this key:-

No.	Common name	Scientific name	Origin
1	Golden Nootka Cypress	*Chamaecyparis nootkatensis 'Lutea'*	North West America / Alaska
2	Common Yew	*Taxus baccata*	Europe / Asia Minor
3	Noble Fir	*Abies procera*	Washington / Oregon
4	Western Hemlock	*Tsuga heterophylla*	Western America
5	Giant Fir	*Abies grandis*	Western America
6	Common Silver Fir	*Abies alba*	Europe
7	Colorado White Fir	*Abies concolor*	South West America / Mexico
8	Douglas Fir	*Pseudotsuga menziesii*	West America
9	Oriental Spruce	*Picea orientalis*	Caucasus / Asia Minor
10	Black Spruce	*Picea mariana*	Canada
11	Mountain Hemlock	*Tsuga mertensiana*	Western America
12	Norway Spruce	*Picea abies*	Europe
13	Scots Pine	*Pinus sylvestris*	Europe / Asia
14	Nootka Cypress	*Chamaecyparis nootkatensis*	North West America / Alaska
15	Lodgepole Pine	*Pinus contorta var latifolia*	North West America
16	Western Red Cedar	*Thuya plicata*	Western America
17	Lawson Cypress	*Chamaecyparis lawsoniana*	Western America
18	Golden Lawson Cypress	*Chamaecyparis lawsoniana 'Lutea'*	Western America
19	Wellingtonia	*Sequoiadendron giganteum*	California

Above and opposite: On the main tower of the Castle is a carving of the Order of the Thistle or the Knights of St Andrew; The Royal Arms of Scotland. This was founded in 1540 by King James V and was created by him, for himself and 12 knights, reflecting Christ and the 12 apostles

The latin motto 'NEMO ME IMPUNE LACESSIT' means literally, 'No one injures (attacks) me with impunity'

Looking towards the Castle from the Rose Garden

The drive leads to the South front of the Castle. The main feature on the South face of the tower is a stone carving of the Royal Arms of Scotland, while on the window-gables between the tower and the entrance porch are six of the badges of Saxe-Coburg in gilt. In the centre of the South face of the entrance porch are the arms of Prince Albert represented in marble. The foundation stone, laid by Queen Victoria on 28th September 1853, can be found at the foot of the wall adjacent to the West face of the entrance porch.

It was from the windows on the West front of the Castle that Queen Victoria in her diary commented on the splendid view up the valley of the Dee. Beneath the small bay windows are the Royal Badges of Scotland and England, together with the Badge of The Prince of Wales, while the bas-reliefs by John Thomas representing St Hubert, St George and St Andrew can be seen beneath the larger bay windows.

The rose gardens on the West side of the Castle, like the other gardens in the grounds, are designed to be in full flower when the Royal Family is in residence between August and October. Sunk in the grass beside the pathway dividing the rose garden is a stone compass positioned by King George VI in 1948. The path leads to a flight of granite steps, finished in 1857 when Queen Victoria noted in her diary that it was 'very fine and such splendid workmanship'. From these steps, shields bearing the Royal Arms of Great Britain and Saxony can be seen on the North front of the Castle, while beyond the sunken garden, which has been improved under the direction of The Duke of Edinburgh, stands the Ballroom. On its parapet is another bas-relief by John Thomas of King Malcolm Canmore presiding over the Braemar Games.

Two hundred and fifty yards along the path to the West are memorials to two dogs: Noble, 'for more than 15 years the favourite Collie and dear and faithful companion of Queen Victoria', who died in 1887; and Tchu, 'a Chinese dog' who was brought from China by The Duke and Duchess of Connaught in 1890 and died later the same year.

The path continues on the line of the granite steps towards the River Dee. About eighty yards along it on the right may be seen flood marks recording the level of the river on various occasions from 1872 to 1937. Opposite these marks on the left of the path is a granite memorial to King George V 'erected in humble loyalty and affection by employees and tenants on Balmoral, Birkhall and Abergeldie Estates'.

To the West of the Castle there is a small Pinetum planted mostly between 1929 and 1933 with a number of well grown specimens, the most unusual of which include *Tsuga mertensiana, Abies concolor, Abies lowiana, Abies homolepis, Abies veitchii, Picea orientalis, Pinus cembra* and *Pinus talmliformis*. In the past few years there have been added *Pinus banksiana, Pinus jeffreyi, Abies sachalinensis, Abies lasiocarpa, Abies lasiocarpa arizonica, Abies koreana, Abies forrestii, Abies spectabilis, Picea orientalis* and *Thuja koraiensis*. These are growing with varying degrees of success in the hard climate.

36

The memorial to King George V 'erected in humble loyalty and affection by employees and tenants on Balmoral, Birkhall and Abergeldie Estates'

Opposite:
Bridge across the
Garbh Alt Burn

Looking west away from Balmoral towards the mountains and the River Dee

HRH The Duke of Edinburgh put the team of Hafflinger ponies together soon after he started driving. The two original Hafflinger mares were given to Her Majesty The Queen by the Austrian government during her State Visit to that country. The other two ponies were their offspring

Opposite: The River Dee - one of Europe's premier salmon fishing rivers

The Queen Mary Garden

On reaching the river, visitors can turn right along the beautiful riverside walk, and after 100 yards turn right again along the path which leads past the staff wing to the Pend Door. On the left at the foot of the road leading to the stables are the kennels, made of cedar. Some were built in the reign of King George VI and some more recently. The stables have mostly been converted into garages, but two remain to house ponies used during the stalking season, and riding horses and ponies for The Queen and members of the Royal Family. Several traps, dog carts and game carts are still used and, together with a four-wheeled Balmoral dog cart made by St Cuthbert's Co-operative Association in Edinburgh and presented to The Queen in 1966, are on display at varying times.

After seeing the stables, visitors who are pressed for time can take the road leading past the game larders and Karim Cottage to the main drive and so back to the entrance. Those with time to spare may care to take the road to the right, which will lead them back to the South facade of the Castle. A short distance along this road on the left there is a small icehouse built into the hillside. At one time it was used to store ice which was brought to the House to preserve meat. Above the entrance door in the East face of the tower there is an inscription commemorating the building of the Castle. Visitors can cross the spacious lawn to find, at a point opposite the tower and about 100 yards from the path, a stone marking the position of the front door of the earlier house, demolished in 1856. Another 100 yards beyond is the charming garden (pictured left), devised by Queen Mary between 1923 and 1925, with a semicircular wall of rocks surrounding a fountain. The gates to this garden bear the monograms GR and MR and were, like the main entrance gates, made by the local blacksmith George Gillespie and erected by King George V in 1925. The Duke of Edinburgh has extended the gardens to incorporate a large kitchen garden. A water garden has been formed to the West of the main garden in the trees between Garden Cottage and the West Drive.

Garden Cottage is where Queen Victoria sometimes used to take breakfast, deal with State correspondence and write her diaries. The first cottage was a wooden building which was completed in 1863 and occupied by a gardener. Two of the rooms were set aside for Queen Victoria and their first recorded use was as an isolation hospital for Queen Victoria's Lady in Waiting who developed scarlet fever in 1864. Alterations were made to the property but by 1894 the wooden cottage had fallen into disrepair and was demolished. The present stone cottage, clad in part with Ballochbuie wood from the forest at the West end of the Estate, was completed in 1895. The interior and exterior of Garden Cottage have altered little despite modernisation and the rooms can be viewed through the windows.

This watercolour of 1882 by William Simpson shows Queen Victoria reading papers at Garden Cottage, being attended by John Brown

The Garden Cottage as it looks today after the alterations and extensions of 1895

From the kitchen garden gate a path leads back to the main drive, by which visitors may return to the entrance. Those who wish to see some of the commemorative monuments should take the right-hand fork at the junction of the roads and walk up to the Golf Course. There have been two additions to these monuments since Queen Victoria's time. A drinking fountain was erected in 1910 as a memorial to King Edward VII; and a sundial made of Caithness stone, given to The Queen and The Duke of Edinburgh as a wedding present in 1947, has been placed near the Prince Consort's statue.

The drinking fountain memorial to King Edward VII

The South Deeside road, which passes through the Golf Course, will lead the visitor past the main entrance with some fine views of Crathie Church across the bridge back to the coach and car parks.

Queen Victoria laid the foundation stone of the present church in 1893 and the building was completed and dedicated in 1895. Queen Victoria's daughters assisted the local community's fundraising efforts by holding a bazaar in the grounds of Balmoral Castle. The present Royal Family have continued the tradition by participating in local bazaars, fêtes and local events.

Crathie Church. A fully illustrated guidebook is available at the church

The Queen and The Duke of Edinburgh have made many changes over the years. In the spring of 1998 the walkway entrance to the Ballroom from the West was replanted with low growing culinary herbs and herbaceous plants gifted to The Queen and The Duke of Edinburgh to commemorate their Golden Wedding by The Royal Regiment of Artillery and The Corps of Royal Engineers.

The formal gardens, covering some three acres, also contain a range of Victorian greenhouses and the conservatory (below), which displays flowering pot plants throughout the year. The vegetable garden (opposite top left), is harvested between August and October during the Royal Family's summer holiday.

Opposite:
Balmoral's greenhouse
and vegetable garden

One
is nearer
God's
heart
in a garden
than
anywhere
else
on earth

Opposite:
Commemorative inscription,
1952 ~ 2002, on panels over
the door of the Conservatory
which was rebuilt in
celebration of The Queen's
Golden Jubilee

A collection of red leather dining furniture and highland dress and regalia is displayed in the large mirrored alcove of the Ballroom

From early April to the end of July, the Gardens and Grounds are open to members of the public. During these times the Ballroom, the largest room in the Castle, houses an exhibition where visitors to the Estate can see paintings and works of art which are displayed elsewhere in the Castle during the Royal Family's residence.

The Old Carriage Hall, behind the Stable Yard Clock, has an exhibition of mounted animals native to the estates, an exhibition showing a flavour of the work carried out by the men and women who live and work on the estate today, and a collection of commemorative china together with several carriages and pony traps.

The boat which Queen Victoria used on Loch Muick, and which was renovated by the apprentices from the Royal Naval Establishment, HMS Caledonia, Rosyth, is also on view.

This collection of ornamental silverware features Highlanders tossing the caber and throwing the hammer. To the right is a Highland Pony carrying a dead stag from the hill

When not in use by the Royal Family or the Estate Staff for banquets, functions and events, the Ballroom houses an exhibition for visitors, of works of art and cases containing interesting items and gifts to the Royal Family from around the world. On the walls are paintings by notable artists such as Sir Edwin Landseer. Famous for his animal subjects and pictures such as the celebrated 'The Monarch of the Glen', he was a great favourite of Queen Victoria and was knighted by her

Behind the scenes

These watercolours and photographs from the archives give a glimpse of the private apartments of Balmoral, now, and how they appeared shortly after completion. Below and on the page opposite they have been arranged to provide an intriguing comparison between the original Victorian decoration and the interiors today. They show how little has changed essentially over the years.

Queen Victoria's Bedroom. Photograph of a watercolour by James Roberts 1857

Below Left: The Drawing Room looking north. Photograph of a watercolour by James Roberts, 1857

Below: Queen Victoria's sitting room. Photograph by Sir Geoffrey Shakerley, 1983

The Upper Landing and Staircase.
Photograph of a watercolour by James Roberts, 1857 (left),
and photograph by Sir Geoffrey Shakerley, 1983 (right)

The Dining Room looking east.
Photograph of a watercolour by James Roberts, 1857 (left),
and photograph by Sir Geoffrey Shakerley, 1983 (right)

The Main hall looking north.
Photograph of a watercolour by James Roberts, 1857 (left),
and photograph by Sir Geoffrey Shakerley, 1983 (right)

The Balmoral Estate

The original Estate of Balmoral, acquired from the Trustees of the Earl of Fife in 1852, extended to 11,000 acres (4.472 ha) of hill, woodland and small areas of tenanted farmland. Over the years up to the present day, the following areas were purchased expanding the area owned by The Queen, in the name of the Trustees, to about 50,000 acres (20,325 ha).

Birkhall was purchased by Prince Albert from the Gordon family for The Prince of Wales in 1848 and passed to Queen Victoria on his death, who, in turn, conveyed it to The Prince of Wales when he came of age, but bought it back again in 1885. The Estate consisted of woodlands, farmland, and hill land up Glen Muick covering 6,600 acres (2,683 ha) and included the house built in 1715 by Charles Gordon. The house was enlarged in the nineteenth century and a substantial wing was added in 1955 to make a house for Queen Elizabeth The Queen Mother after the death of King George VI. A modern kitchen and staff dining rooms were added in 1981 designed to blend in with the older building. The house has an exceptional garden reaching from the south of the house down terraces towards the River Muick.

Dalliefour was purchased from James R Farquharson of Invercauld in 1868 at the same time as the balance of a 999 year lease was bought from the Marquis of Huntly.

Ballochbuie was purchased from the Laird of Invercauld in 1878 to prevent a large area of Native Caledonian Pinewood being sold to an Aberdeen Timber Merchant. The area of woodland and hill extended to 6,420 acres (2,610 ha) and now forms the West End of the Estates. The Pinewood has been preserved by successive generations of The Royal Family and now contains one of the largest remnants of the old Caledonian Pine Forest left in the country. Regeneration trials in the early 1970s established a 50 acre (20 ha) regeneration block which is growing well. This has been greatly extended to encourage the natural re-generation of the Pine Forest.

Bachnagairn was purchased in 1947 by King George VI from Colonel Eric Mackenzie of Glen Muick to protect the South end of the Estates. It consisted of 6,720 acres (2,732 ha) of good quality, high hill land containing the source of the River South Esk and running down to the top of Glen Clova to the South. To the North it bounded with the Whitemounth Beat rented from Abergeldie which, in turn, lay to the South of Ballochbuie, and Lochnagar. There was a good stand of quality larch trees surrounding the site of the burned down Lodge which blew down in 1975. In 1985 The Prince of Wales got volunteers, interested in the area much used by hill walkers, to erect a windmill driven electric fence around the woodland site. This has encouraged very satisfactory regeneration of larch, birch and rowans for the benefit of everyone. The fence was removed in 2004.

Brochdhu is a 37 acre (15 ha) piece of land opposite Birkhall House on the East side of the River Muick consisting of a bank of mixed woodland, a small croft, two cottages, the local School and the East bed of the River. The disposition dated 19th July 1948, simply states that the Subjects had formed part of Birkhall Estate for upwards of 40 years but, as no title had been granted, Colonel Mackenzie was remedying the defect before selling the rest of Glen Muick Estate.

The Spittal of Glen Muick was purchased by King George VI from Colonel Mackenzie in September 1948. It extended to 7,720 acres (3,138 ha) of hill ground, very peaty in part, between the County of Angus boundary on the East with Loch Muick and Bachnagairn to the West and South. This area together with Bachnagairn had comprised the whole Estate of Bachnagairn as it used to be in 1862 when owned by Donald Ogilvy of Glen Clova. It also laid the foundation for the sole ownership of Loch Muick on the subsequent Whitemounth purchase. The Superiority of Whitemounth was owned by the Marquis of Huntly who feued (rented) it to the Gordons of Abergeldie. In 1885 Queen Victoria purchased the Superiority which included the 'Right of Hunting'. In 1950 King George VI purchased the feu from Mr Bertram Fuller Gordon. The area extended to 4,250 acres (1,727 ha) of high hill ground running down from Lochnagar and the Dubh Loch area to the north side of Loch Muick.

In 1997 a further 3380 acres (1,374 ha) in Glen Dell were bought from the Earl of Airlie to allow better control of the Red Deer on the Bachnagairn beat. The very old drove road, known as Jock's Road is included in Glen Dell.

Delnadamph is situated on Upper Donside, West of Cockbridge, on the famous Cockbridge to Tomintoul Road some 16 miles north of Balmoral. The previous owner, Mr Freddie Stockdale divided the Estate into 2 parts. In 1977 he sold the Grouse Moor on the basis of 1,587 brace of grouse and 26 stags on 6,700 acres (2,724 ha). The purchase was made to provide driven grouse shooting once The Royal Family had given up the tenancy of the Invercauld Grouse Moors of Corndavon, Micras and Gairnshiel.

In 1980 the balance of the Estate was purchased after it had been on the market for some time. It consisted of the Lodge, a small let farm and some very poor young conifer woodland - an area of 967 acres (393 ha) in all. The Lodge was in poor condition with 2 major structural faults and was demolished in 1989. The total area of 7,667 acres (3,117 ha) is on good quality hill land. The numbers of grouse dropped to below 400 brace immediately after purchase, but with good keepering, the bag came up to over 1000 brace in 1990 and reached 1206 and a half brace in 2003.

The Queen, Prince Philip and The Prince of Wales take a close personal interest in the running and improvement of the Estates. Run in conjunction with them are the sportings on the neighbouring Abergeldie Estate of approximately 12,500 acres (5,081 ha) which have been leased from the Gordon family since Queen Victoria's time.

The majority of the Balmoral land is hard, heather clad hill ground overlying granite with small areas of more fertile land along the south bank of the River Dee, which forms the northerly boundary, and along the west bank of the River Muick which forms part of the East boundary. This better land is used for farming and forestry. The ground rises very steeply in parts from 656 feet (200m) at the junction of the 2 rivers and 919 feet (280m) at Balmoral up to 3,789 feet (1,155m) at the top of the Lochnagar massif which dominates the whole area. The weather conditions can be very severe, particularly in winter when snow can come to the high ground in October and still be lying in north facing corries in July. The average annual rainfall is 33½ inches (85mm).

The nature of the ground and the climate restricts the use of the land. Farming is difficult and all farm and young forestry ground has to be surrounded by a 6 foot (2m) deer proof fence as protection against marauding deer. There are 2 small let farms with the rest of the farm land used for grazing and making winter keep for the Highland Cattle, ponies and deer on the Estate. The Queen is Patron of the Highland Cattle Society and founded the Balmoral Fold in 1953. The Fold has enjoyed considerable success exporting cattle to Germany, Austria, Holland, Belgium and Denmark until cattle exports were stopped by the BSE ban. The Fold produced the Champion Bull at the Oban spring sales in 1988, 1989 and 1990 and the Female Champion at the autumn sale in 1990.

Above (clockwise): A horse clears redundant fencing from the pine forest. Traditional fencing is a highly important aspect of capercaille conservation, and its ancient forest management. A capercaille. A Caledonian pine stands sentinel in heathland dotted with birch

Below (clockwise): Members of the Balmoral red deer herd in velvet. Pony-trekking is a significant part of the Estate's outdoor leisure facilities. The Estate's highland cattle are not only highly picturesque, but also contribute towards the Estate's revenue

The Highland, Fell and Haflinger ponies are kept to recover the Red Deer from the hills during the stalking season (below).

They are also used for Pony Trekking, and for taking the Public around the Policies on a carriage during the Public Access season. A team of Fell stalking ponies is driven in Combined Carriage Driving Events by Prince Philip during the summer.

There are some 7,200 acres (2915 ha) under trees including the fine specimen trees along the Main Drive, the Native Pine Wood in the Ballochbuie Forest, and an area of 2,200 acres (890 ha) at Birkhall let on a long lease to the new Forestry Commission in 1932 with the lease bought back in 1985. The Ballochbuie provides shelter for Red Deer and other areas of woodland are opened up to the Deer as they become mature. The management of the game resources of Deer, Grouse and Salmon fishing are very important providing employment and earning revenue as well as providing enjoyment for successive generations of The Royal Family.
Grouse are shot mainly on Delnadamph but also elsewhere on Balmoral providing good quality driven shooting. The salmon fishing has a relatively short season this far up the river from the sea with the best time from May to June. All sportings not required by The Royal Family are let on the open market.

One of the main problems facing the Estates in the twenty first century is the increasing public demand for access to the countryside which involves pressure on privacy, traditional land uses, the wildlife, the sportings, and general amenity and severe erosion of hill paths combined with the problems of litter, fires and uncontrolled dogs.

Red deer are managed to keep their population in balance with their habitat including their wintering range. The deer cull is often difficult to achieve in the area as a whole, due to difficult terrain and open winters in the last few years. The majority of the venison goes for export to Europe. Interestingly, the red deer herd in Windsor Great Park was established with Balmoral stock.

Opposite: red deer stag

Balmoral in winter

Balmoral and the surrounding area is arguably as beautiful during the winter months as it is during summer, albeit not quite as accessible. Winter conditions can prevail on the summit of Lochnagar during any month of the year. Some of the wildlife such as the mountain hare, the ptarmigan and the snow bunting are only resident in this unique part of the British Isles.

As the days grow shorter the mountain hare's coat turns from mottled brown to pure white

A cousin of the red grouse, the ptarmigan, is only found on the high barren mountain tops

Loch Muick

The Lands of Glen Muick

The name Glen Muick in Gaelic acually translates to 'Glen of the swine'. And Muick, is pronounced 'Mick'.

The area around Loch Muick and Lochnagar is managed, like the rest of the Balmoral Estate, with the highest environmental standards in mind. The Estate's Ranger Service, based at the Spittal of Muick is grant aided by Scottish Natural Heritage and assists visitors and hill walkers in this wild and remote region. Queen Victoria was an enthusiastic and regular visitor to the glen and one of the cottages was once used by the Queen herself. The lodge at the far end of the loch was built by Queen Victoria shortly after the death of Prince Albert. This lodge, the Glass-alt-Shiel, and other cottages are still used today.

The Spittal of Muick was once home to crofting families which welcomed the passing cattle drovers making their way to the lowland markets. The word 'Spittal' means hospice or resting-place in Gaelic, and the original building provided a stopping place for the drovers. As well as cattle the route over the Capel Mount to Glen Clova was also used regularly by whisky smugglers and soldiers trying to catch them. As communications improved these isolated communities died out and the Spittal ceased to function in the mid-1800s.

The lands of Glen Muick were from an early period under the Mormaor of Mar, and later the old Celtic Lords of Mar. In the 13th century the Bisset family became landlords as the Crown Vassels to the Scottish Kings, but were followed by the Frasers before the lands were passed by marriage to Sir William Keith,

Great Marshall of Scotland, in 1351. They later became the property of the Earl of Huntly and Aboyne, and then James Farquharson of Invercauld before being bought by Sir James McKenzie in 1863. He was a silk mercer who bought Glen Muick as a sporting estate and added Bachnagairn. This beat, the Spittal beat and the White Mount beat were added to the Balmoral Estate between 1947 and 1951 by King George VI. There are many low and high level walking routes in this area. Over 120,000 people visited The Spittal of Glen Muick in 2003. The Upper Deeside Access Trust, is a non profit making environmental charity which was established in 1998 to give vital support to the maintenance, development, and understanding of countryside access. The work is funded by Aberdeenshire Council, Scottish National Heritage, Scottish Enterprise Grampian, The Cairngorms Partnership and Balmoral Estate with shared objectives in protecting the natural heritage, providing for public access and sustainable economic development.

Very little has changed since Queen Victoria's time and it is hoped that the isolation and wild beauty of Loch Muick and Lochnagar will continue to be conserved and managed for future generations to enjoy. However, as visitor numbers continue to increase each year, the Estate and its ranger service must find ways to allow estate activities, recreation by visitors, and conservation of the landscape and wildlife to co-exist.

A young golden eagle

Wildlife

MAMMALS

The area around Loch Muick and Lochnagar is notable for red deer, but other mammals are much harder to see. Roe deer, foxes, mountain hares, red squirrels, stoats, OTTERS, mink, moles, voles, shrews, woodmice and bats are all found here. Rarities also include the PINE MARTIN and the WILD CAT.

Because of predation by introduced mink and loss of habitat, the water vole is Britain's most rapidly disappearing mammal. However, it is thriving high up in the watercourses at the head of burns around Glen Muick. Over 40 colonies of this rare mammal have been discovered by Researchers from Aberdeen University in recent years.

MOUNTAIN HARES are found on the moorland and as high as the Lochnagar plateau. They are difficult to see as they are mostly nocturnal and are also well camouflaged. A good time to see them is at dusk when they start to graze, and after dark on the road down the glen. Look out for them on winter days when there is no snow lying and their white coats make them very conspicuous. Mountain hares are the main prey for golden eagles. Foxes and stoats also prey on the mountain hare.

RED SQUIRRELS live in the woods, but they are more commonly seen lower down around the River Dee. They are difficult to spot as they spend most of their time up trees - look out for bits of pine cone raining down from high branches. They live here all year round and do not hibernate.

STOATS are present but rarely seen. The stoat's winter coat (sometimes called ermine), is completely white except for the tip of its tail, which stays black. In their summer coat they are sometimes confused with squirrels. They move very fast, weaving amongst trees or in and out of stone walls, so it can be difficult to get a good view of one.

The area has two species of deer: the more commonly seen RED DEER and the much smaller ROE DEER. Red deer can often be seen near the Spittal of Glen Muick, but otherwise they tend to spend summer high in the hills. The roe deer can be spotted in woodland.

OPPOSITE PAGE:

1	Black Grouse	8	Dotterel
2	Otter	9	Golden Plover
3	Merlin	10	Capercaille
4	Stoat	11	Pine Martin
5	Dipper	12	Red Squirrel
6	Common Lizard	13	Wild Cat
7	Adder	14	Red Grouse

BIRDS

The upper area of the glen from the Spittal (420 metres) to the summit of Lochnagar (1155 metres) is mainly moorland. Most of the birds are summer visitors or true migrants.

The meadow pipit is probably the most common small (sparrow-sized) bird to be seen on the open moor. The wheatear arrives from Africa around the beginning of April. This bird perches on lookout stones and is easily alarmed. All wheatears have an obvious white rump, which makes them easy to identify. Another moorland bird likely to be seen near the loch is the ring ouzel. This mountain blackbird is closely related to the garden blackbird but has a pale crescent shape on its breast. It is secretive and often its presence is advertised by the male's churring call before any sighting is made.

RED GROUSE are the game birds of the open moorland. Listen for the "go back go back" call of the territorial male. The red grouse found in Glen Muick tend to be the dark variety, which can lead to confusion with its larger cousin the BLACK GROUSE, which can also be found feeding in the open moorland. The black grouse male is a metallic blue-black in colour, the female or grey hen, is more difficult to identify - look for the white wing-bar and the fork to the tail. The extremely rare and endangered CAPERCAILLE is unique to this part of the British Isles, and only seems to flourish in ancient Caledonian Forests. Despite its large size, it is a highly secretive bird and difficult to see.

The group of birds called waders are well represented in the glen; most arrive in the spring for the short breeding season and are gone by August. The orange-billed oystercatcher and the lapwing, with its distinctive crest, are the most successful of the group. The CURLEW is also commonly heard, in flight and whilst nesting on the boggier areas of the glen in the spring. Others, including the GOLDEN PLOVER, redshank and dunlin have declined in number over the last two decades. Goosanders are regularly seen on the loch, a recent survey showed between 59 and 63 pairs in the River Dee catchment. Because they eat trout and salmon, goosander numbers are controlled by licensed shooting.

The peregrine falcon, one of the fastest-flying birds in the world

Two pairs of red-throated divers feed on Loch Muick and nests have been found in the area. Occasionally we are graced by the appearance of a great northern diver or 'loon'. In 1996, black-throated divers were seen on Loch Muick. It will be interesting to see whether they will be regular summer visitors or decide to breed in the area. The fabulous osprey is often seen diving into the loch during the summer.

DIPPERS are common on the streams, unmistakable with their dark brown and white coloration. They feed on aquatic insects in the stream bed and their presence is a good indicator of un-polluted highland streams. Grey and pied wagtails are also found feeding on insects by the waterside, but they lack the aquatic skills of the dipper. Birds of prey are well represented in the area. GOLDEN EAGLES hunt the moors and are spectacular birds with a 6 to 7 foot wingspan. Each pair will have a territory of about 90 square kilometres. Buzzards are now common on Deeside, but are more likely to be seen in the lower, wooded parts of the glen. PEREGRINE FALCONS have become more numerous in recent years. Their streamlined shape and screaming voice is often encountered on the circuit of the loch. A smaller falcon, the MERLIN, occasionally arrives in the spring with the wheatears and meadow pipits. It nests on the ground and feeds on small birds and large insects.

August and early September is a quiet time as most of the summer visitors have gone, but autumn brings in more birds from the north. Whooper swans fly in from Iceland and huge flocks of thrushes, redwings and fieldfares come from Scandinavia. On Lochnagar you will see the Arctic grouse, the ptarmigan, hidden amongst boulders and blaeberry, but rarely seen below 2000 feet. Two unusual birds of the high mountian plateau are the DOTTEREL and the snow bunting. Unlike most other birds it is the male dotterel that incubates the eggs and rears the young. The female will lay several clutches of eggs with other males. After the breeding season the dotterel will migrate back to Africa where it spends the winter. The little snow bunting on the other hand, spends the whole year high up on the plateau. In winter it forms large flocks of up to 500 birds and these flocks are regularly seen being blown about like little pieces of white paper near the summit of Lochnagar. Due to the presence of these two species Lochnagar has been designated a Special Protection Area.

Please minimise disturbance to these birds by keeping to the recognised routes and keeping dogs under control and on a lead at all times.

REPTILES AND AMPHIBIANS

The ADDER is the only wild snake you will see in this area. Although it is poisonous it is shy and will not strike if left alone. It has a distinctive V or X marking towards the back of its head and a dark zigzag running along its back. Adders are cold-blooded creatures. They have to absorb heat from their surroundings to stay active, to do this they bask in the sun on warm surfaces - this is when people usually see them. The common frog can be found throughout the area as can the common toad, which is regularly seen around Glen Muick. The more secretive COMMON LIZARD is usually seen during the summer months.

Map of the Policies

 Monuments   Estate Roads

Walks around the policies

You are welcome to try these walks which provide short but interesting routes through fine countryside. Please keep dogs on a lead!

Deeside Walk - *YELLOW ROUTE*

A short, easy, level walk around the cricket pitch returning along the river bank to the tea room. 1¼ miles. ½ hour

Mountain view walk - *RED ROUTE*

Beginning with a winding climb to the first cairn viewpoint above the Castle and river valley, the route takes in a fine view of Lochnagar (1155 metres). 1¾ miles. 1 hour

Castle view walk - *GREEN ROUTE*

After a short climb to the Castle viewpoint, this fairly easy walk levels out and gives fine views of the castle policies and the Dee valley. 1¾ miles. 1 hour

Three Cairns walk - *BLUE ROUTE*

Starting with a steep incline, this walks levels off towards John Brown's statue then winds uphill, passing Princess Louise's and the Purchase Cairn, returning via Prince Leopold's Cairn. 2 miles. 1½ hours

THE COUNTRY CODE

PLEASE
- remain on the paths.
- close any gates behind you, or leave them as you find them.
- keep your dog under control and on a lead.
- consider others.

PLEASE DO NOT
- feed or disturb the deer.
- drop litter.
- camp overnight.
- light fires or carelessly discard cigarettes.
- remove or pick any flowers and/or plants.

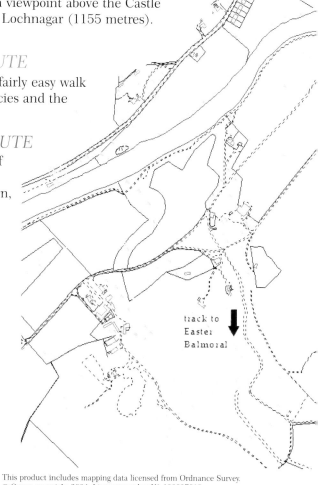

track to Easter Balmoral

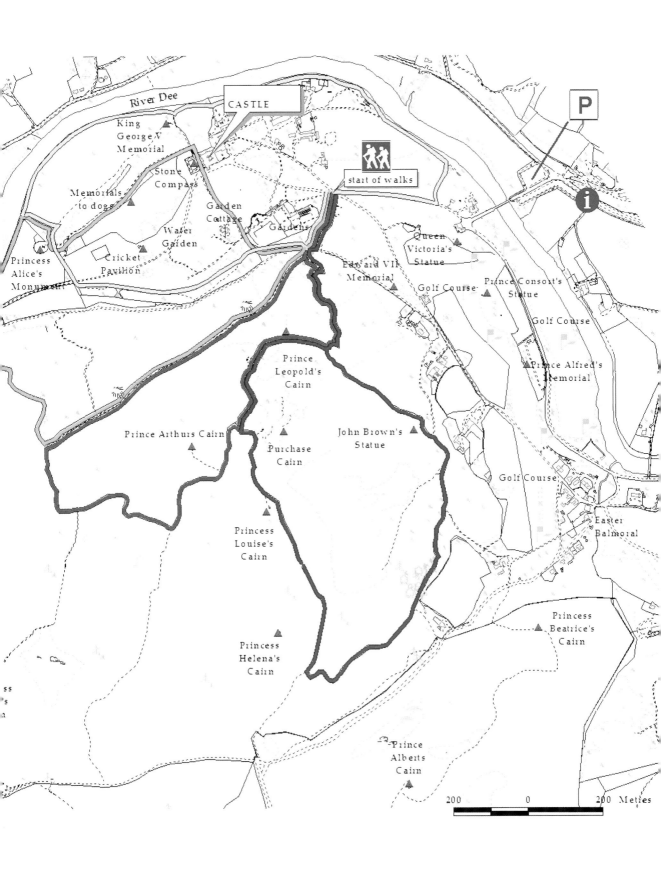

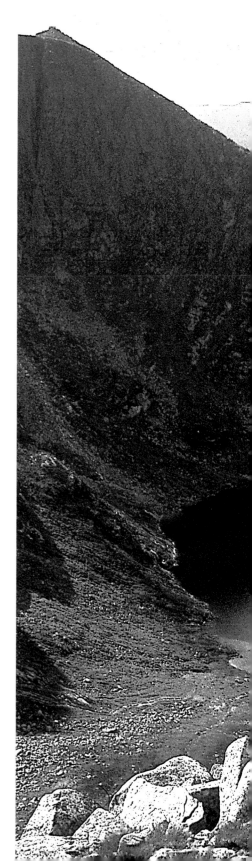

Designed and edited by Nick McCann

The publishers are grateful to the writers of previous guidebooks
to Balmoral and to Neil Cook, Polly Freeman and Claire Bird,
authors of the booklet Loch Muick and Lochnagar, 1998

All wildlife photography by Mark Hamblin of Carrbridge,
unless otherwise credited

Published and produced by Heritage House Group.
Ketteringham Hall, Ketteringham,
Wymondham, Norfolk NR18 9RS
Tel: 01603 813319 Fax: 01603 814992
email: publications@hhgroup.co.uk

© HM The Queen, Balmoral Castle 2011

91976 - 02/11